Bob's Shorts

Or, do you have to be old
to wear shorts, drink beer
and tell short stories?

Bob Harner

"Bob's Shorts. Or, do you have to be old to wear shorts, drink beer and tell short stories?" by Bob Harner. ISBN 978-1-63868-223-3 (softcover).

Published 2025 by Virtualbookworm.com Publishing Inc., P.O. Box 9949, College Station, TX 77842, US. ©2025, Bob Harner. All rights reserved.

Bob's Shorts?

This is a narrative collage of humorous, nostalgic stories from when I was around 10 years old. I have also dedicated this work to my wife, Beth, who has put up with me for more years that I can count or know, (but don't tell her that). These stories are about some of the true events and some which were stretched a little that happened over my beginning years since I've been around on this rocky mess that scientists call earth. Think about this – I'm old now, I'm allowed to forget and if I cannot remember then I am allowed to make things up, right! Come to think of it, it's just like that old TV show, when it started you heard, *"My name is Friday I'm a cop – The names have been changed to protect the innocent."* Hmm, wouldn't you really think that some of those people are happy that their names were changed?

Things happen in life that people just shake their heads at and others shake their fists. I hope you just grin or get a chuckle or two. Well anyway, let me tell you some of my stories when I was about... eh, well... when I was not so damn old.

Contents

Restaurant Days

I grew up during the 1950s in Southeastern Pennsylvania, just outside of Philly, in an area that they should have named Pennsyl-tuckey. The area didn't really have a name but we did have three paved roads, the rest were just stone covered or that other stuff, (you might know it by its technical name, DIRT). Our homestead was in Bucks County between the towns of Warrington, Warwick and Warminster where to my knowledge there were no important war battles of any kind or for that matter any battle at all. So, come to think of it there might have been some yelling or maybe a feud or something but I doubt it.

I never asked why each town's name started with the word war but maybe our founding fathers or maybe some village idiots just liked to pick fights?

By the way, getting back to the story, like I said before when I was around 10 years old, my folks owned a restaurant in Warminster called the Warminster Restaurant, (Now that took a lot of thought to name it that). My brother was a part time soda jerk, my sister stayed home playing with her dolls and of course me who always thought that up until I was about 14, my name was, "You little bastard."

Being the youngest and of course the smartest, that's right, the smartest, because my old man actually gave me an official title for the job I did at the restaurant. He called me his Manager of the Environmental Sanitation System, better known as "MESS". Hey, it's a title isn't it? Of course, you may have figured out what that actually meant, I didn't get it for a while, remember I was only about 8 or 9! Here's something relevant to that, I was also the only one in that department! My duty was that I had to drag out the garbage. Most of it was too heavy to pick up, so when I attempted to throw it in the dumpster most went on the ground. Yuk! Just more smelly trash to pick up! At least it was only on Saturdays, but then again, when it was summer and I was out of school, I had that marvelous prestigious position every other day of the week, Sundays was reserved for God but I'll tell you about that later.

My Old Man was a pack rat - nothing was ever thrown away when he was around because as he often said there was always a use for everything. One day he found an old wooden mop handle in the shed out back, What he did next was, he drilled a hole in the end of the mop handle, hammered a nail in the one

end of that wooden shaft, cut the head off the nail and ground it to a point on the end with an old rusty file.

"Wow! You made me a spear." That was all I said and he growled something and looked at me over his glasses. Then he gave me an old burlap potato bag and I was told, "Kid, starting today and then every other day in the morning, I want you to go around the parking lot and pick up all the trash and dump it in the dumpster around back."

But knowing how smart I was, he added, "Keep the bag and your stick, don't throw them in the dumpster - you'll need it the next time you have to do your job."

So, the day came and the trash was picked up, thrown in the dumpster around back. The bag and my stick with the nail that was hammered in one end then filed to a point were put in the storage shed out back, Ta-Da, done to perfection!

As far as I can remember, the old man always said there were never any dumb questions asked, only dumb answers. So just to prove to everyone why I think I was the smartest kid that ever fell off the back of that proverbial turnip truck, I asked my old man, "Pop, so why do I have to carry the stick with the nail that you stuck in one end when I pick up the trash around the parking lot?" "You don't really think that I have to fight someone off with my stick with a nail in one end for trying to steal our trash, do ya?" "But don't worry, I did figure out what the burlap bag thing was for – that's so after I catch the trash stealing thief, I put his sorry ass in the bag, tie it and throw him in the dumpster bag and all …. right?" Just about then, my father just looked at me, over his glasses, shook his head, walked in the kitchen and yelled something at my mom about your son goes to church every Sunday and all he wants to do is to kill people? Hmm, maybe I must have missed something about the part of my brother killing people?

When we were out of school during the summer, the three of us kids were told to eat lunch and sometimes dinner at the restaurant. A few days or maybe weeks later, who knew how long, hey, it's a warm summer day without school, no clocks, no calendars, NO FREAKIN' SCHOOL HOMEWORK! All I can remember is it was on a day that ended in the letter 'Y'.

One day I found out from my sister, miss nosy one, that our folks hired a new waitress at the restaurant. (Aha! Another chance at screwing with a lesser intelligent being.) Now picture this, there I am sitting on the end stool at the counter and out of the kitchen comes a beautiful long haired blonde girl with a tight sweater, a pair of blue jeans that looked like she painted them on and a little apron tied at her waist so you could see better that tight sweater. Opps! Did I mention the sweater before? Her name was Babe, Belle or maybe Beauty or even Tight Sweater or something like that. Actually her name was Bertha and was in her early twenty's. Wow, this will be an easy mark, you know, blonde with big "Waazoos", (Ahh, I wasn't allowed to say tits or boobees back then), even though I think she may be a bit too old for me maybe just a couple of years. But, I'm in love, whatever that meant? She comes over to me and in the sweetest voice, "What'll it be, Big Guy?"

After a big deep breath and with my best imitation of Humphrey Bogart was when I blurted out my answer, "I think, I'll have a cheesesteak with fried onions, pickles, ketchup, French fries, a black and white milkshake, and a piece of lemon meringue pie, doll face."
"Do you have money to pay for your order, sir?" I then gave her one of those seductive smiles, with one eyebrow lifted and the best accent once again I could mustard, "Of course I do Toots, I got enough to buy this whole hash house! Besides I even know the owner."

And then that beautiful piece of womanhood goes to the doorway of the kitchen, "Mrs. H. there's a kid out here with a bad Humphrey Bogart accent that ordered a cheesesteak with

4

fried onions, fries and a black and white shake." "I asked him if he could pay for his lunch and he said....."

"Whoa! Wait a minute ..... KID!" "Did she say kid?" Well, that was the end of that romance right there and now, and to think it just took that one little three-letter word, KID!

The report from the kitchen was, "Wait a minute does he have on a dirty, wrinkled tee shirt like he slept in it for a couple of weeks, shorts, untied beat-up sneakers, no socks, sporting a crew cut on his almost white hair and a tan like a construction worker?" She turns, looks, "Ahh..." My mom as usual pokes her head out of the doorway and with a smile, "That's my youngest, give him the blue plate special - meatloaf, mashed potatoes and green beans with a glass of MILK."

"Oh damn! Another 'Blue Plate Special', not even a glass of freakin' chocolate milk or even a crumb from one of those free donuts she gives to the cops!" "Just a Blue Plate Special."

Just like in the old silent films where Black Bart tied Nell to the railroad tracks and the Northwest Mounties saved the day....

" Curses, Foiled Again!"

The Old Man & Me
Down at the Ball Park

As far as I can remember my father was only a little taller than my brother, my sister or me, the shrimp. He wore glasses, was a little heavy set, going bald and oh yeah – CHEAP! The last couple of years he was around he took my brother and me to Shibe Park, better known later as Connie Mack Stadium down at 21st or 22nd and Lehigh Avenue in Philly, which was the professional baseball park for the Phillies, that I guess was named after some old guy named Shibe who was around before baseball was a sport. Anyway, at one time it was the home to the Athletics, Phillies and even the Eagles. Later the A's moved to Kansas City, the Eagles moved to Franklin Field down at the University of Pennsylvania and the Phillies in 1953 changed the name from Shibe Park to Connie Mack Stadium for some other guy who probably grew up with Moses.

Sorry to get off the track. The key word here was "CHEAP"! Anyway, the old man took us there and the our Old Man, my brother and I always had to wait outside the park until the second inning or maybe the third was over then go get the tickets which were regularly $2.00 for adults and 75 cents for

6

kids under 12 or 13. Wait a minute now, that was the normal price but after the third inning it was 50 cents for adults and kids under 12 or 13 were FREE with a paying adult. But, they were whatever was left but mostly 'restricted viewing' seats!

"WAIT A MINUTE NOW!" "I have a question?" "Why did I always get the seat right behind those damn poles?" "I don't know, did I actually like professional baseball?"

I remember this one time, just the Old Man and I went one summer day in 1957 when the Phillies were playing the NY Giants at Connie Mack Stadium and of course, I'm right behind that damn foul pole, again! As far as I can remember this was the last year the Giants were based in New York before the big move to San Francisco. I am almost sure that Willie Mays was at bat. Then there was the pitch, the crack of the bat, the white rawhide orb screaming towards us and hits the foul pole about ten or fifteen feet above me! The roaring crowd is on their feet – the ball clangs when it hits the pole – the ball comes flying down on the fair ball side and hits my old man right smack on top of his freaking head! His hat flies off onto the steps. The crowd was roaring, some fat guy sitting behind us was laughing so hard he spilled his beer all over himself plus two other guys. Another guy was waving his arms trying to catch the ball and knocked over the hot dog man. It was just like that saying when the Hindenburg Zeppelin exploded, "Oh the humanity!" Think about it, there is my old man's hat sitting on the step full of hot dogs, sauerkraut, mustard and beer in the heat of the afternoon sun. The hot dog man, the fat guy and two other guys were yelling at each other while rolling around in the slop on the seats and steps. All of this and my old man rubbing the top of his head and with a tear in his eye staring at his soggy, smelly hat getting stepped on now. Well, that's when I knew the meaning of life! I'm starting to really LIKE professional baseball!

That wasn't by far the best part of the game. The best part of that game was just a couple innings later with Richie Ashburn of the Phillies proved how great of a hitter he really was and actually while we were there made history. He hit the same spectator twice within the same time up at bat. His first swing at the start of the inning was a foul ball. It went screaming over the Phillies dugout and struck some woman in the face while she was talking to someone and I think it might have broke her nose. Just then the whole crowd went wild, yelling, screaming, wooing and howling. Then, after everyone calmed down, he hit the next pitch, a second foul ball that hit the same woman while she was being carried from her seat by two ushers. Maybe that was his ex-old lady or something like that, who knows? After all that hoopla, the Phillies went on to beat the New York Giants 3-1 and the old man was still rubbing that big lump on the top of his head. My opinion of all this was, NOW I totally LOVE Professional Baseball and I'm really into it!

All the way home in the car the Old Man kept on mumbling while rubbing his sun burnt head, "Lord, why didn't my youngest kid catch that ball, he had a glove with him?"

I finally answered him, "Because the freakin' pole got in my way!" He never took me to another game, he said something about me and a bad luck omen. I still love Baseball and the Phillies won!

Oh yeah, I forgot to tell you about on the way home in the car, I gave pop back his hot dog, sauerkraut, beer soaked, smelly hat and that's when I think he actually started to cry or at least maybe he shed a tear.

Me & Pop
Gone Fishin'

Did I ever tell you about when my old man took me fishing? Ahhhh, our first big day of father and son bonding, just him and I. My brother told him he didn't want to go cause he was going to help mom open the restaurant so therefore I would go with him. Yea, happy days, oh what joy! The only good part of this story is that I got to sit at the front window seat of the old Ford – Yahoo! I got the ultra famous shotgun seat for once! As I recall it was on a Tuesday afternoon when pop told me we are going fishin' early the next morning because Wednesdays was the slowest day at the restaurant.

"Cool beans!" "I don't have to pick up the trash with my burlap bag and carry the stick with a nail in one end that was sharpened to a point around the parking lot at the restaurant!" Wrong! Before I could even smile about that he told me we'll be back early enough and I can pick up the trash afterwards. Oh will happy days never end! (Little bit of sarcasm there people). He also told me to dig up some worms over by the cesspool because they were the biggest, juiciest and tastiest worms of all. Whoa - first of all, visualizing about what he just said in his last sentence, really, I could picture the old man saying they were the best and tastiest – how did he know? Did he or someone ever take a bite out of …. Get that thought out of your mind! I've been fishin' before but if your worms came from there – THEY FREAKIN' STINK! I went to the trash bin and found an old Campbells' soup can for the worms' new home. That soup can was still a little dirty, but HEY, the worms came from the cesspool, this has to be an upgrade for them, right?

The next morning the old man gets me up before our neighbor, Mr. Monte's chickens were crowing, but that is another story for another time. "Why we getting up so early Pop?" the old man snorted, then looked at me over his glasses one more time, "Cause by the time you get your lazy bones out of bed the fish will have already eaten their breakfast." The only thing I could think of but dared not to say to him with that look on his face, "What's wrong with being there for their lunch hour break?"

Ok now we're up and ready, we load up the old Ford with the rods, the reels, tackle box, a couple bottles of soda for me, a thermos of coffee for him, ham and cheese sandwich for him, peanut butter and jelly for me, a hand net to bring the big fish in with, stringer to put the fish on. Oh, of course an one old empty,

dirty, onion bag, which I did not have the slightest clue why and the most important article, his lucky hat that has his fishing license pinned to it. He says it is his lucky hat because he forgot his license one time and the fish warden fined him $6 dollars and 50 cents when the license only cost $3. Oh, the horror – a minus $3.50, Cheapo! So now the license is always pinned to his hat that sits on his balding head so he don't get sunburn on the chrome dome.

We're off, headed to Churchville Reservoir an enormous lake about 30 – 35 minutes away. We came down this winding road full of trees and all of a sudden there it is. Wow! It looks like the whole freakin' ocean to me, I can't even see the other side but then again it is still freakin' dark out. The road stretches out straight as an arrow for what seems like miles with the lake on both sides. I'm hyped! Look out Momma we're bringing home a fish dinner! Then it occurred to me, "Hey Pop, why did they put the road across the center of the lake?"

With a big grin on his face and by thinking that he finally got me, "You see, that's so that when you fish you can always have the wind on your back by which side of the road you choose."

"But Pop, the fish live in the water they don't care which way the wind is blowing, do they?"

"Shut up Kid, you're going to scare the fish!"

By now the Sun is just starting to come out when we are crossing the lake when I noticed all the fishermen only on one side of the road with their lines already in the deep. Could it be that my old man and all fishermen in the known free world knew something magical about this lake or just a lucky guess, hmmm, did he actually get one on me? Hmmm maybe, but he did have his lucky hat on.

Now we drive all the way across this reservoir and there is a parking lot on the other shore where he parks and we start to unload our gear - the rods, the reels, tackle box, a couple bottles of soda for me, a thermos of coffee for him, ham and cheese sandwich for him, peanut butter and jelly for me, a hand net to bring the big fish in, stringer to put the fish on, and of course an empty onion bag, which I still did not have a clue why. Now we haul all this stuff about a quarter of the way back down the road that goes across the lake until he finds the ideal spot that seemed to me to be a 4 hour march. He stops with a, "This is THE SPOT!" It has three big flat rocks for us to put our stuff.

First he puts my sodas in the onion bag and tells me to put the bag in the water. Ah-ha, I got it! It was to use the cans of soda for chum to entice the fish! If it was to entice the fish I should put the thermos in there too, right! I'll just let him figure that one out himself. All he did was grab his thermos and shake his head while looking up at the sky mumbling that same old saying of his, "Oh Lord, why me?"

I now think it would be a good time to ask a logical question, "Hey Pop, why didn't we just drop off our stuff here instead of lugging it back down here when we passed it once but parked all the way down there?"
"Shut up kid, you're going to scare the fish!"

Now we settle down on a some big flat rocks get our poles and stuff ready when.....
"ROBERT!" He only calls me Robert when he's really mad, "Where are those WORMS?"

"Ahh, in the Campbells' soup can."

"And where is the can?"

"By the cesspool where you told me to dig them up." "I really didn't know what you wanted them for."

Now his face turns the color red that I have never seen even on ripe tomatoes, Santa Clause's suit or even a candied apple. He looks straight out upon the lake while gritting his teeth and says real slow, "Go back to where we parked the car, and see if you can find some worms under some leaves, rocks or somewhere!"

I don't know how long it took me but I was only 9 or 10, didn't have a wristwatch to watch the time it takes me and to tell the truth I do get a little distracted sometimes. Anyway I'm back and the old man has calmed down and casting out a lure like the rest of the men around us. "You were gone close to an hour, did you find any worms?"

"Only a couple baby ones." "I did catch a couple of grasshoppers on the way back here."

Now all the big-time fishermen up and down the lake are laughing, pointing their finger, shaking their heads while mumbling something about taking kids fishing and of course, grasshoppers. And there I am, humiliated, laughed at by all the people in the wide world of fishing. Now my dignity and reputation ruined but what they don't understand is they don't stand a chance against the best thing in the whole world, a smart kid! I reach in my pocket get a special, stupendous grasshopper out and on the hook he goes. Now all the worldly fishermen are watching, snickering and getting ready to start laughing again when I haul back and let it fly. It was the best cast of my entire life into the lake of shame and possible defeat. – first to hit the water was the grasshopper still on the hook, then the bobber. WOW! A perfect cast all of about 15 to 20 feet, what a perfect cast! Suddenly I realized that my bobber as soon as it hit the water it had to sink, oh damn, after a cast like that and now I need another stinking bobber – reel it in. HOLY WHALE-POOP! My line goes straight, the pole almost breaks in two and I'm being dragged into the lake! All the fishermen cheered, and in unison yelled, "They're hitting on grasshoppers!" They were all running around like a bunch of ants on a dropped lollipop to get their free grasshoppers!

Meanwhile, I'm in the fight for my life or maybe this big fish's. It's me against the Loch Ness Monster and maybe his whole family. I was thinking about the way it must had been the same as Captain Ahab against Moby, you know, boy do I have to spoon-feed you? Moby Dick, yes the great white whale, oh yes he's big. My mind is racing as much as the line he's pulling off the reel. My old man is yelling at me to tighten the drag – It just flashed into my brain, now I know what my stick with a nail in one end and filed to a point is actually used for – it's, it's a FREAKIN' HARPOON! Why, oh why didn't I bring it!

The drag is tight, all of the local fishermen are gathering and old Moby Dick himself comes to the surface beckons at me for the first time. In my eyes he is every bit of 40 feet maybe could be a 100 feet long. He beckons the second time then the third. I see his cold dark eyes looking deep in my soul. I give him one last tug and drag him on the rocks. My old man grabs him measures him and hollers out like the town crier, "My Kid just caught a 21 and a half inch carp on a grasshopper!" Twenty one and a half inch carp, he has to be mistaken for sure, we're talking whale size, you know, Moby Dick size!

So now all the fishermen sighed, sat down and put their lines back in the lake.

Wow what a rush! After all that fuss I'm looking at my pole, the carp and the old man and... Oh my god, there's a tear rolling down the old man's cheek. "You all right, Pop?" He sniffed, wiped his tear and looked out on the water. It seemed that with all the commotion his famous lucky hat with his license on it fell off of mount baldness and is now floating on the water about 15 feet and the slight breeze is taking it farther away. But, that is not the worst thing to ever happen in a person's lifetime. IT'S STARTING TO SINK! ... And the second worst thing or I may have that fact backwards to happen because walking down the road toward us, is the Fish and Game Warden!

How can anyone really believe a story something like this? — The old man explaining to the Warden about the worms left at the cesspool, the grasshoppers everyone laughing at, my 10 or 15 foot cast, while holding my 21 and a half inch carp, and of course telling him about his lucky hat where his license is at the bottom of the lake, while turning looking at me then the Warden, then back at me gritting his teeth. The warden looked at me then the old man, the lake and then back at me, then my father still holding the carp, "Yup, fishing without a license, that will be a $6.50 fine."

Then after handing pop the ticket the warden tells him, "Well have a nice day but remember no more fishing until you get a license."

I really don't know who was more proud and happy, the old man or me? He told me, "We will take the carp home and give it to Mr. Monte so he could use it for his garden."

Wait a minute! Wait a minute! Wow, I couldn't believe this - was my school teacher ever wrong, she told me fish come from eggs, now the old man says you plant them in the garden and grow some more carp.

Then with a big smile, I told him, "But I was thinking I could get my fish stuffed like you got that pheasant of yours." Then he tried to tell me that people don't get a carp mounted to put them on a mantel over the fireplace.

After that entire hullabaloo, I only have one question about the events of that day, if you lose something like a lucky fishing hat that is suppose to be lucky - is that still lucky or is it called irony or maybe its an oxymoron?

Mr. Monte

or what is better known as the "Strawberry Caper"

Lets talk about Mr. Monte. Well he was sort of a kind old man who lived next door to us but then again anyone over 20 is old to me. Anyway old man Monte lived with some old nasty, always yelling, bitchy old woman that he called his loving wife. Actually they lived on the street behind us and owned the big field to our right if you looked at our house from our street. He planted the field each spring with what he called vittles.

That's when I found out what vittles actually were. Cabbage, lettuce, green beans, peas, corn and you know that other stuff your mom made you eat so you could have dessert. Anyway, I called him kind because he always planted about 4 or 5 rows of strawberries next to the fence by the side of our house, yum!

By not getting off the subject, this is one of the things I learned from my brother that I had to swear to, that I would never tell our blabbermouth sister or anyone else in the world for fear of torture, death or even going to an all girls' school. Usually by the end of April just about dark my brother and I would go out by the shed, burn a cork on one end and then rub it on our faces and hands.

Why do you ask? It's camouflage! Our faces darkened along with black or dark colored tee shirts, and dark hats. We were the **CRISPY-PLATOON**, better known as the Commando Raiders of the Infamous Strawberry Patch Yahoos.

Our mission was then to sneak around our house and onto the enemy's front line of defense, the fence. Now, this is where my brother, Slick Hal, tells me he's too big to get under the fence and only I would be able… well it didn't take that long to figure that out but I did realize that every time I would come back with some berries I would dump them in a big pot then go for more. Each time when I came back with another batch they were GONE! "Ahh, hmm, the rabbits got them – I tried to fight them off but there were too many!"

Now wait a minute, I'm not that gullible, I know something about rabbits because on the end of our street lived old man Fritz who raised rabbits but he called them hasenpfeffer or something like that because he always said, "My English no too good cause I come from old country".

Fritz showed me all the different types of rabbits he raised, like white ones, brown ones, gray ones and even mixed colored ones. He even had different sizes with some small and some big ones that were almost as big as me and I couldn't even pick some of them up. Some were so big that I thought they were crossed bred with kangaroos. As far as I could tell I didn't know what he did with all of them. My brother once told me he ate them but I never believed him.

So now after a while of the raid on the patch the lights came on the back of Mr. Monte's house and we could hear that old witch, "Those damn kids are in the garden again – get your shotgun – I'll teach those little bastards a thing or two!"

We ran down the fence line across the street and into the woods. When we stopped I asked, "Well, did you save any strawberries?"

"Ahh, a long pause as he wipes the strawberry juice off his face, Ahh NO, remember I had to fight the rabbits?"

Right then it would normally be a fist fight with him and me, but since he could kick my ass it was, "Mighty big rabbits eh?"

When we got home our mom was waiting for us and politely says "And where have you two gentlemen been all dressed up like bandits?"

The first thing that popped in my mind was, "Oh just playing around, you know guy stuff, army stuff."

"I heard you two army men were in our neighbor, Mr. Monte's, garden again feasting on his strawberries!"

The first thing out of Hal's mouth was, "It was his idea, mom." Boy, talk about getting thrown under the damn school bus! I just closed my eyes and waited for the smack. BUT WAIT, to my surprise, no smack – no yelling only both of us were told to go get a bath then come down here and sit at the table then think of a gift to buy Mr. Monte's wife for taking the strawberries and to get a basket of strawberries for Mr. Monte.

"Now you two Army men will pay for this out of your own allowance."

I'm sitting there thinking to myself, "What the hell just happened? First, before she changes her mind, think of a gift!"

"Mom I got it!" "We can get the old hag a new broom so she can fly around the neighborhood on Halloween!"

Mom just looked at me, put her hand over her mouth and ran in the other room.

Getting Restaurant Stuff

One day the old man said that he had to go pick up some stuff for the restaurant because they couldn't deliver it and needed some help to go get them. Then said that my sister, Oggie, and I had just volunteered to go and my bother had to help Mom at the store. Wow! That was a blatant lie. I never to this day ever volunteered for anything. Anyway after questioning his remark about volunteering, he only said to shut-up and get in the car.

We left at daybreak that day on our adventure of that perilous journey not knowing if any would survive the onslaught of shopping for, and I quote, "Stuff". At first, we were headed north into farmland because once you see those little red signs along the roads you know you're in farm territory and of course the cows and other animals give it away too.

The first group of those red signs we came across my sister reads out loud; first sign, I proposed to Ida. Second sign, Ida refused. Third sign, Ida won my Ida. Fourth sign, If Ida used. And the last piece of wisdom on that last sign was BURMA SHAVE. Then Oggie looked at me, "Those signs didn't make any sense, who is the other Ida?"

After about an hour drive we get to this other sign that said Grange Fair and pointed to this little road. I guess we were there because the old man went "Whew, almost missed that turn!" By the way, the sign took up the whole side of some farmer's big barn and the arrow on it was bigger than our car.

After going through some trees it opened up to like a big field with tents and open buildings and wagons, some more tents and some more buildings with no walls. They had pigs in pens, horses tied up, goats, sheep and even cows on the other side of the fence. Every place you looked there were men with beards dressed in black with funny black hats selling all kinds of stuff what our neighbor, Mr. Monte, would called vittles. They even talked different then us by saying things like thou, thee and thy.

Pop probably had a list of stuff to get cause he went right to this one man and the man told him to bring his car around and he'd load him up. Hold it! You mean to tell me that our old man, the senior Deacon of a Reformed Baptist Church, is doing something sneaky or maybe illegal? "Pop, I don't want to get arrested, you know with the stuff you are going to buy and I figured it out the reason you got her and I to come along with you because a cop would never stop you on the way home if you had little kids with you, right?"

He just shook his head and looked up at the sky, "Oh Lord, why me?" " This man is going to load the car so we don't have to, okay?"

The guy puts a big sack of potatoes in the trunk along with this big sack of corn that still had to be peeled and in our ice chest that we brought he loaded with these slabs of meat but he called it bacon, didn't look like bacon to me, but... Then in a box he had a big bunch of green stuff and something that looked like red stalks of celery, and before I could say anything the old man said, "it's rhubarb for strawberry / rhubarb pie."

On top of the whole mess the guy placed a big tray of strawberries, (Now I know why my brother didn't come with us)! He closed the trunk, and on the back seat set this enormous basket of peaches. Then off we went back to civilization, you know like places that didn't smell like the ass of a cow or you didn't have to worry where you stepped.

It was a great ride back to the restaurant because I was up front in the shotgun seat once more and my sister was in the back with the peaches. "Daddy, can I have a peach?" "Sure sweetie, give us each one too, will you please."

It makes me mad and confused that he was always nice and polite to my sister, Oggie, but all I got was the look. Anyway, there we were driving back and me sitting in that seat, eating the juiciest, sweetest peach that I ever had in my entire long life of 9 or 10 years, (Its hard to remember things from so long ago).

The trip was basically uneventful except when we got back my sister told my mom that she didn't feel well and mom asked her what did she eat; she told her about 10 peaches. With that mom looked at her arms and her back and ..., "Oh my, no more eating peaches for you little girl, you got hives."

Mom made her some stuff that she put some powder in a glass, some liquid and stirred it then made her drink it. Oh my God, I thought my sister was going to die right there. Her face turned more colors then all the crayons in the box and mom told her she can't go outside in the sun for a day or two then took her home. After they left my brother came over to us and asked me what all the commotion was about.

About the best I could tell him was, "Mom said Oggie ate a whole bee's hive with some peaches or something like that and took her home probably to get some honey from her?"

Country Style
Sandlot Baseball

Next door to us on the left side of our house was a field and then after that was where Ralph and his family lived. He had a younger brother and a sister whose names I never did care to know because they were way to young like maybe 5 or 4. Anyway, there was this field between our houses that Ralph's father would cut the grass to make our ballfield and that's where during most of the days in the summer us guys in the neighborhood would play baseball, girls would watch if they wanted and even played if we were short of players. Sometimes we didn't have enough kids to play ball so if we were one less to make up a team we would eliminate left field if a left handed batter came to the plate. If he hit it there, it was an out and the opposite with a right handed one. We had to make that rule because out of all the guys only Ralph was a southpaw.

Any kid from about 8 to about 15 could play and we would chose upsides every day. At least I was not the last one picked. Another rule was if the team on the field didn't have enough players for a catcher the batting team had to catch but nobody was allowed to steal home. Oh yes, one last rule and the most important that nobody liked was if you hit the ball over towards the cesspool you had to go get it yourself. Yummie!

One day we got together, set up the rules, picked the teams and started a game. I was pitching and Ralph was the first batter. When the first pitch was thrown right down the middle all you heard was the crack of the bat and the ball was on it's way to being a home run until the miracle for any pitcher happened! The cover on the ball came off and the ball just dropped into Jimmy's P's glove. "YER OUT!"

"NO I AIN'T!"

Then the argument was the ball was not the same as with the cover on it. Then we all looked at what was left of the ball in Jimmy's glove. Back to the argument that the ball was still caught so it was an out. Then we all looked at what was left of the ball in Jimmy's glove once more, noting that now it was only a ball of wound thread one size smaller of about what it was originally. Ralph said we could get some vinyl electrical tape and tape it like new. Then we all looked at what was left of the ball in Jimmy's glove again. I told that's no good because the last time I did that my old man kicked my ass for using all his tape. Then we all looked at what was left of the ball in Jimmy's glove once more and wondered if it was actually an out or not and we didn't want to wait until we went back to school in the fall to ask Mr. Hamilton the Little League coach.

After doing this with different reasons why this was an out or not, trying to decide what to do next and looking in Jimmy's glove we came to the solution – we flip a coin, heads its an out and tails a fair ball! Rats! Nobody had a coin. Then I had the idea of going to the restaurant, get a soda, get a coin, make the decision and continue tomorrow. Everybody, all 7 of us liked my idea especially about getting a soda was the greatest idea since like ever!.

We got in the restaurant I went to Mom and told her the problem about our game plus our request. "A soda for everyone and a coin?"

After telling her the event of the cover of the ball coming off and Jimmy catching what was left. Plus our decision to flip a coin but nobody had one. "Well, I don't know, I know since you boys want to gamble by flipping a coin to see who wins - we'll flip for the sodas too!"

We all looked at each other and then Jimmy said, "Wait, if we lose we ain't got no soda."

Mom grinned with "That's 'We don't have a soda.'"

Jimmy replied again, "Yeah, ain't got no soda none, we're thirsty, look we are all goin to drop over dead. We might as well go back to the field and get a drink out of the cesspool.

While just shaking her head Mom reaches in the pocket of her apron and pulls out this big shiny brand spanking new silver dollar coin. Heads you get sodas and tails you don't and flips it. Everyone looks at that shiny piece of silver floating up in the air-twirling end over end, sparkling like the fireworks at Willow Grove Park.
When just then my old man reaches out and catches it! That's right the old man, my father, my flesh and blood grabbed it — Mom looks at him, "Give me that coin!"

"But we can't teach our youngsters to gamble, remember in the Bible it tells of the Romans gambling under Jesus's cross at Calgary Hill."

"GIVE ME THAT DAMN COIN!" The old man gave it to her, turned around and walked into the kitchen.

She turned to us, told us to sit in the tables in the corner and went and got us each a ice cold bottle of Hire's Root Beer and best of all she had one too. Then she whispered to us, "We all needed a BEER after all that, eh boys."

We all clinked our bottles together, laughed, drank our sodas and laughed some more. But as we were all walking home, we never really decided if Jimmy was actually called out or not.

About 2 days later mom gave me a special red box that only had the word Wilson printed on it and in the box wrapped in tissue paper, was a brilliant white ball with red stitches on it, whoa, a brand new official Major League Baseball for us and told us to never say another word about who or where it came from.

About three or four days later Jimmy hit a foul ball and you guessed it right! There it went in all its glory and shiny white cover with its red stitches on it, right in the cesspool!

I think that might have been a moral to this but I guess you can say it was Jimmy who either Christened or maybe BATH – TISED our brand new baseball!

Our Vacation Road Trip:

Better known as The Cabin that will live in Infamy!

Everybody was pumped up, our folks were closing the restaurant for two weeks and we're going. I was not told where but mom packed me a jacket, (maybe a skiing trip?), swim trunks, (maybe the lake or shore?), and a bunch of other clothes which I don't care about. We loaded the brand new car I'll never forget, an aqua and cream painted 1955 Oldsmobile 88 mom bought and stuffed all of the luggage and a big ice chest in the trunk. And there away we went!

Somewhere around noon we stopped for lunch at this old farm style place with all these men wearing black pants, white shirts, suspenders and funny straw hats. The women and girls wore dresses and these white little things I guess were called bonnets on their heads. They even talked a little funny too. Most different was they rode around in these horse and buggies – no cars. Hmm, I must have fell asleep in the car and we're in a different country, probably somewhere like Canada or maybe the North Pole where I could meet up with Santa's elves, they are the same size of me right?

Inside this barn styled building we sat at this long table with people that we didn't know and waiting for something to happen. Then all of a sudden without warning they started bringing out these big bowls of food, I mean BIG BOWLS of food and platters of fried chicken, ham, turkey, even some stuff I had no idea was except one thing hot dogs yeah I love hot dogs. My brother nudged me and said they're sausages, I told him no they're not, its not breakfast time now. So, I took a hot dog anyway but I don't really know what it was then but I do know what it is not and it's not a hot dog. I asked Mom how do they expect us to eat all this food when they keep bringing more? Everyone laughed, (about what – who knows?). When no one else could eat anymore they served us something called shoo-fly pie! "That's it!" "No Way am I going to eat flies especially some that were in some farmers old shoes!"

And as this goes on, none of us could walk right because being so full we waddled like ducks, I mean we were to full to even burp. So, back in the car once again and we drove until dark and finally we pulled into the Famous Log Cabin Lodge. Well, that's what the sign said that it was famous but not what it was really famous about. To me it looked like we were in Sergeant Preston of the Mounties' Yukon Territory.

They had these little log cabins built like in a somewhat circle, (I guess in case of an Indian attack). We got the one that was set back a little more than the rest. I guess that was for we were the first to go in case of those Injuns, you know, gulp! Before I went in I found a big stick. My sister asked me why did I have the dirty old stick and of course I told her. "You know – the Indians and bears and of course maybe even Big Foot!"

"Mom!"

Mom pointed at me then the door and only said one word, "Stick!"

There we were in the back woods of Davy Crockett country in a little log cabin with no protection. This cabin was so old that it was probably built by Davy Crockett's great-great grandfather maybe even someone before Christopher Columbus got here. The cabin had basically two rooms plus a very small bathroom. Actually, there were two bathrooms one inside and one in a little shack outside that really stank. Also in the cabin there was a small room with just a bed in it with a blanket nailed over the doorway for a door I guess and the main room had a fireplace, two sofas, two chairs and one plain light bulb hanging from the ceiling by a wire. In the corner of that room was a cabinet with a cast iron frying pan and pot hanging from it. There was no stove there but a couple hooks hanging in the fireplace. The main room also had a door to the backside of the cabin along with the main entrance and a widow with no screens. Outside the back door were a fire pit and a picnic table. Hmmm, so it was the pioneers who invented hot dogs and hamburgers. All this and I almost forgot, came with a view of a small pond that

had a great big sign with big red lettering reading - NO Fishing, NO Swimming, NO Hunting, NO Hiking, NO Nothing!

Now, let me tell you the way I figure this could happen; if a bear comes walking by, you run around the cabin get my stick that I was rudely told to put out there, come back and hit that furry bastard over the head. Then start a fire in the fire pit with my wonderful stick that I had to raced around the cabin to get, skin the poor bear with your bare hands and roast him over a two foot diameter fire pit so all can feast on him at the picnic table with all the freaking mosquitoes feasting on us. Boy, what fun!

Now my old man got us all together to show us about the bathroom even though only one could get in there at the same time. I think I was 10 about then, I should know what a bathroom is used for. Trust me, I never saw anything like that in my life. First, in this little closet of a room was a little galvanized metal sink that only held about a quart of water. A half of a regular toilet, a wooden barrel strapped to the top of the wall a bunch of pipes with valves and little signs on the valves. Most important was this shiny brass chain hanging down out of the top of the barrel with a wooden doo-dad on the end.

"Demonstration time" – My Father said he used to be a plumber a long time ago and knows all about this type and how it works. He starts with the explanation that you do your business. You turn on the big red valve down the bottom which gives everything water then turn on this blue valve with the arrow pointing up to the barrel or tank, that's what the pros call it, which will fill when you use the pump handle with a lot of force to fill the barrel.

When the barrel is fill the water will come out of this little pipe into the toilet now its ready and you can flush the toilet by pulling the chain.

He pulls the chain with the wooden thing-of-ma-gig on the end that breaks off right as it comes out of the barrel! He looks at the chain with a wooden thingy on the end in his hand. Then we all look at the barrel up on the wall, and then look at the chain with the wooden thingy on the end in my old man's hand. This was at the same time we all put our hands over our mouths so he couldn't see us laughing like hell.

"I can fix this!" Mom told him she would get the man at the office, "NO, I'll get this", as my old man grinned and stuck out his chest.

So then he stands on the toilet with the little pipe squirting water in the bowl but still can't reach the barrel so when he's stepping down off the toilet the most dreadful thing happened, you guessed it - his foot slipped and went into the toilet! My sister held her ears for the words coming from his mouth but the rest of us were laughing out loud! My mother said she would get the man at the office again,

His only real words were "NO" as he pulled his foot out and decides to climb onto that flimsy little tin sink to get to the barrel. Now wait a minute folks this is just like on the radio – "And now the rest of the story!"

Here is a man about 5 foot 6, 270 pounds going to climb on a tin sink that probably couldn't even hold me. Anyway, he's back on the toilet then the sink, reaches over to the barrel where the brass chain was .....
OH MY GOD!!! ... the sink breaks off the wall, the old man falls to the floor with the other foot in the toilet now, the sink hits the main big Red valve and breaks the valve off while there is water shooting all over the place and with the pipes broken here comes the barrel of water falling right on the old man's bald head! Mom rushes out to get the man from the office while

34

my old man is rubbing his head with one hand and holding the brass chain with the wooden watcha-ma-call-it on the end in the other.

My sister asked me what happened and I turned to her, looked her right in the eye and told her, "Just wait till you see how we have to take a shower!"

Very, very, soon afterwards we left the Famous Log Cabin Lodge with the owner of the cabins hollering and cussing at Pop about some law suit and that he will not get his money back for the cabin and some other stuff that I can't repeat, but if I told anyone what was said I'd get my ass kicked and soap in my mouth.

Then in a cloud of dust and a hardy "Hi – Yo – Silver" we are back on the road again. But went about a half of a mile then had to make a U-Turn cause he went the wrong way.

Just to be nice when we went pass the Famous Log Cabin Lodge once again I saw the man from the office was still in the parking lot jumping up and down while running around, waving his fist at us and still cussing at pop.

So, I think I was the only one who waved back a hello at him while he started to throw stones at us.

Bob Harner

Just a Hole in the Ground

The Skyline Drive in Virginia or better known as a skinny, very windy road that wanders on top of this mountain where you can't see anything because of the fog in the valley. That's it, like I said before, we traveled most of the night and the next day down this very winding road and stopped at this parking lot they named after some person that actually could see through the fog and mist, His Lookout Point. Actually, we still couldn't see anything even from those telescope things that the Old Man was very reluctant to put a whole nickel into. Therefore back in the car we go with the decision to head back on route and go to our next port of call. Up ahead there was this small old wooden sign that obviously somebody handmade but didn't know how to spell too well which read, "GO DIS-WAY".

Believe it or not the old man sees this little sign and made a command decision, "We're going to the Skyline Drive Caverns."

Whoa, you mean just like in the book my class in school had to read, "Journey to the Center of the Earth"? "Cool!" as I told my sister, "Just like in that movie, we'll see monsters, and fight some other creatures and stuff!"

36

All she said was, "OOO, Pat Boone was in that movie."

When we got there Mom asked us all quite a few times does anyone have to go to the bathroom because it's very chilly down in the cave and everyone put on a sweater or jacket. Look at me what a dork, a sweater on and wearing shorts. Then Old Cheapo Pop told me if the Park Ranger at the gate asked me how old I am to just hold up six fingers and don't say a word because I could pass because I was so short. My answer to that was "Why?" "Sure, you want me to LIE so it's free for me to get in and you don't have to pay but I'm the one who will be struck by lightning, and not allowed through the Pearly Gates and spend like forever in HELL!" Now Mom's looking at me over her sunglasses, the Park Ranger is looking at Pop and he's just grinning and wiping the sweat from his forehead.

After the My Old Man paid the Ranger for ALL of us we each were given a ticket went to the entrance where about a dozen people were standing around. This is where another Ranger asked for my ticket, ripped it in half, gave me the stud and told me not to lose it and if I did I couldn't come out and be stuck in the cave forever.

Everyone laughed but me. I didn't think that was funny at my expense, but wait which would be better? In the cave or Hell for the rest of eternity? Now, while I was thinking of that Mom looking at me in particular asked again if anyone had to go to use the bathroom again.

Then a lady Ranger came up and told us her name was Patsy or Patty or maybe Peggy, I wasn't sure, and also told us that she was our guide. If we had any questions to just ask her in the mean time let's get started on our tour and follow her. Then we started down this tunnel for a long way, turned a corner and it opened up to a big what she called a gallery. Oh yes, Ranger Petunia I guessed that's her name was telling us about these things hanging from the ceiling that looked like icicles dripping water were called one thing and these things on the floor was where the water was dripping to were called something else. There was water dripping and gurgling everywhere and then she said the whole cavern stays right around 55 degrees all year long. Yes, even during the winter snows and summer heat.

That was about the moment I raised my hand, "Yes, and your question is, young man?"

"I got to go, NOW!"

This is all while my legs are crossed and me doing the pee-pee dance, Ranger Pamela, (maybe that's what her name was), tells us, that the only restrooms are at the beginning of the tour or at the end and she thinks that we are probably closer to the beginning. While she is in her looong tour guide mode, my eyes are even crossed now. Mom tells my brother to take me back so I can go. He comes back with let Oggie go with him and points to me and our sister. Mom told him to go!

"Oh, okay and then, let's go, squirt" ….

"I don't have too now!" was all everyone heard as they looked down and saw me standing in a yellow puddle. They gasped with their mouths wide open and then LAUGHED and I mean they all BIG TIME EMBARRASSING LAUGHED!

Oh, the anguish, the humiliation, but now at lest I felt relieved while standing in the puddle of embarrassment.

Mom grabbed my hand said to all that I just got over being sick. Whoa, wait a minute my Mom lied for ME! My Mom actually lied for me – kinda makes it all better now. At least I won't be alone in Hell. We marched back to the car got some clothes, got cleaned up, changed and went to the gift shop which also had a little cafe in it. We both got hot fudge nut sundaes. My Mom lied for me! Isn't life great? Mom likes me but to tell the truth Mom and I really hate those freaking holes in the ground!

Now the rest of Our Wonderful Vacation Trip
Or the Vacation of Horror!

Still on our family vacation, the next day as we were driving down the road Pop says, "We're getting close to the beach now, you can start to smell the salt in the air, Arrrr, Da Briny Deep!"

Good Lord, I guess he thought he was once a pirate? All I could smell was the swamp we were driving through to get to the, "WAIT A MINUTE, POP SAID CLOSE TO THE BEACH - YAHOO"

I'm starting to actually enjoy this endless trek of Hillbilly Redneck Heaven. Up ahead was a signpost 'Ocean City, Maryland, only 20 more miles. Wow, we are going to the ocean with the roaring surf, the boardwalk with all the amusement rides and of course, the beach with all that sand up the crack of your ass.

After about an hour of driving down the wrong dead end streets we pulled into a parking lot and some guy told Pop, "2 Bucks."

The old man started digging in his pocket and gave him the money when mom grabbed his arm pointed to a sign that said 'FREE PARKING'. Pop turned to tell the guy something but he was about a half a block away laughing while running away from us waving Pop's two bucks in the air. I Think I actually saw steam come out of the old man's ears.

Our orders were to get your bathing suits and we will go across the street to the bathhouse to change. Now that's an experience worth writing a whole book about. It had cold-water showers, lockers and towel rentals plus old men looking at all the young boys. We changed, put our clothes in a bag to take back to the car because Pop was to cheap to spend an extra 50 cents for a locker while he's still mumbling about the 2 bucks to park.

Mom rented a big beach umbrella and we all marched down to the briny deep. The sand was so hot I thought my feet were going to cook when my brother told me, "Get used to it, Hell's like that, but a whole lot hotter!"

Wow, that was the first time I didn't have anything for a comeback and while looking at him was, "Least I won't be alone!" Then with a cloud of dust he kicked sand at me.

We set up camp, so to speak, spread out a blanket, our ice chest, some towels and of course the rented beach umbrella with a hole in it as big as Pop's bald head. Now the old man is gritting his teeth mumbling to my mom why didn't she check out the umbrella before she rented it? Her response to him was short and sweet, "SHUT UP!"

I could just about hear the Old Man still mumbling about the two dollars to park and now he adding that he will probably have to buy that vender a new umbrella because SHE didn't check it out that it had the hole in it before renting it.

Mom and us kids are now attacking the surf while the old man is sitting under the umbrella. Oggie is in water up to her knees and lets out with a big scream, "Something just rubbed up against me!"

I thought it's probably a whale but then it attacked me, I reached down and grabbed it's green slimy flesh with all it's tentacles and hoisted it out of the deep blue sea. It was a monster or how about a big clump of seaweed! What do you do with it? You throw it at your brother, right, he ducks and wham! Right in my sister's face. She yells, "Mommmmmy!"

"Leave her alone you two and Oggie you come over to the other side of me." Now you know when you are growing up there are little things that sometimes piss you off like when she went around me to get to Mom she stuck out her tongue and put her thumb to her nose while wiggling her fingers. No respect like someone else used to say! There will be revenge.

Well after a while of getting beat up by the waves with sandy, salty water in every orifice in your body, plus your eyes are burning and you're shivering cold, YOU ARE TIRED! We're headed back to the blanket. "Whoa! Look at that, it's a beached whale!"

"Be nice that's your father and ... (a little chuckle) .... the sun moved, now he's asleep and he's not in the shade of the umbrella."

There he was, in all his sun-burnt glory. His front of his legs, his stomach, his chest and of course his bald head, all in the color of a bright red candy apple you get at Halloween.

Well, we are packed up and on the trek back to the boardwalk when Mom mentions she has to turn the umbrella back to the rental place. Pop starts mumbling again about we'll probably have to buy the guy a new umbrella because Mom never looked and saw a hole in that one. She gives the vendor the umbrella and the first thing he does is opens it up and looks at the hole.

That was when the rental guy says to Mom, "Ahh, here's the one with the hole in it." "You know, I told that kid of mine not to rent this one out." "I'm very sorry, here's your rental money back, I don't rent junk out like that." "As a matter of fact here is my card for a free rental the next time you come down plus your rental fee of $2.00 back." Mom thanked him and just smiled at Pop.

Next stop is into the showers where the water is piped in straight from the North Pole up where Santa and his elves live plus where old men watch the young boys coming out of the showers.

About a hour or so later we pulled into the parking lot of Captain Barnacle Bill's Seafood Emporium and Fishing Pier. Then came the question of all questions when I asked Pop, "Do we have to pay to park here?" Everyone told me to shut up and I think I may have seen steam come out of Pop's ears again.

Everyone got whatever they wanted and I got some Blue Point Crabs. Whoa, they were 3 monsters, I mean I never seen ones that big in my whole life.

I proceeded to pick one up and finally get even with my sister when Mom told me to put it down, you don't play with your food. Then the waitress came back and tied a bib around my neck and gave me a little wooden hammer.

The nice waitress then showed me how to break a claw off this bad boy, tapped it lightly with the hammer and used a little itsy-bitsy fork to get the meat out. WOW! I am now a connoisseur of Maryland's Blue Crabs.

I also came to know why they gave us a bib because you can have a ball with a hammer and a crab to beat the stuffing out of especially when your sitting next to your sister who doesn't have a bib!

Scooters?

For those who can remember these machines and I almost can, it was a Cushman Scooter that my brother got when he was about 15. I don't remember if he saved up the money to buy it, the old man loaned him the money or mom bought it for him but I think the last scenario is right. Anyway that doesn't matter, this story starts with my brother and some friends of his getting some rusted hunk of junk that had a flat tire, torn seat, a couple of dents, a bent headlight shell with a broken bulb in it off the back of a pick-up truck. They also unloaded 2 old wire milk cartons full of old spare parts, plus a big cardboard box with other spare junk parts in it. I guess I don't know what it was but it was in desperate need of some paint. Then they all pushed it over towards the shed, talked about it some more, then waved and they all left with just Hal and I looking at it.

"What is it?"

"That my little brother, is a 1948 model 48, 2 speed, 6 horse, walk through, kick start, Cushman Scooter."

"Damn squirt, you don't know nothing."

"I know TWO things and one thing is that this is a pile of freakin' junk and two I doubt it will ever run."

So, every minute of spare time was wrench clinking, screwdrivers driving and a lot of hammer banging going on but after a while I have to admit that an old rusty scooter came out of the shed puffing away like our old lawnmower. TA-DA!

"Whoa Nelly, Look at that!" "All it needs now is a paint brush!"

A couple of days later there was a roar coming up the road like a roar I never heard before. There was a humungous cloud of dust maybe even a tornado or hurricane or maybe the beginning of the Great Dust Storms of the 1930's that we read about in school. Or just maybe it was 10 or could it be 100 scooters. Oh My GOD, My brother is in an outlaw scooter gang! Wait a minute, they are freaking scooters not motorcycles! Nobody looks like Marlon Brando from the movie, "Wild One". Ok, they are just a few friends of my brother going for a little ride. After asking if I could go, I hear, "No way Jose, you cramp our style, Daddio!" Whatever the hell that meant.

Style he said, maybe they're going to get matching leather jackets, engineer boots or even tatoos? Hal and his buddies took off in a cloud of dust and a mighty .... forget that last thought .... I went over to the restaurant and had some lunch.

After finishing my make-believe cheesesteak with fried onions, pickles and of course French fries which was actually the world famous blue plate special, meatloaf, mashed potatoes with gravy and string beans, again, a Hatboro cop came in and asked for my mom. Oh-my-god, she's getting arrested or maybe she didn't give him some donuts with his free coffee this morning? You see, all the cops from the area know that mom gives them all free coffee and donuts every morning. Maybe I'll be a cop when I grow up! I could probably get a whole breakfast FREE! I do know the owners, right? Hey! Anyway let me get back to my story!

I didn't quite hear it all but I know it was something about my brother being locked up in the penitentiary or in with the gangsters on death row and mom had to make him his last meal or something like that. And then, the dirty copper took my mom away! Anyway, about an hour or so later Mom comes back with my brother and asked the Hatboro cop if he wanted anything to eat and gave my brother lunch. Whoa, hold your bladder sissy pants! Did he get the blue plate special? <u>HELL</u> <u>NO!</u> He got an unbelievable cheesesteak with fried onions, pickles, French fries and a black and white milkshake.

Mom goes in the kitchen and I get on the stool next to Hal, "Ok, guy what did you get busted for, you know, like thrown in the big house?" "How much was your bail?" "After the trial how much time you gonna get?" "What brand of cigarettes you want me to bring you when you're in the slammer?"

"Listen squirt, I was not charged with anything just a warning, no bail, no trial and I don't smoke."

"But...."

"I was riding on the street, I don't have a driver's license and my machine broke down."

"You mean if that bucket of bolts didn't break down, you would have had the cops chase you and your blood thirsty gang out of town?"

"You're an idiot!" "I got a warning from the cops and Mom had to come pick me up and have Hank from the gas station across the street haul the scooter home."

After all of this hullabaloo, everyone should know that this world is completely screwed up because lets face it - it is upside down. Think about it, the bad guys, you know the gangsters, murderers, hooligans, they get a cheesesteak with fried onions and a pickle, French Fries with a black and white milkshake and a piece of pie or a big grilled cinnamon bun for desert. But, us good guys that are angels from heaven, the salt of the earth, get a platter of pig slop like freaking meatloaf, mashed potatoes and string beans and a glass of milk – not even chocolate milk!

Hi-Yo Silver!

A friend of mine, Jimmy, who was about 1 or 2 years younger than me had a brother, Joey, that was my age who couldn't hear or talk too well but was learning how to sign at a special school he went to in Philadelphia. They lived down the end of our street just a half a block opposite Fuzzy's Auction House and Junk Emporium where they sold used junk. Inside there was also this big room with a stage at one end where every Saturday night Old Fat Fuzzy would auction off his junk. They also had some other people selling more junk in the other part of the building. Some of the stuff that the other people sold was neat but most wasn't. There was a man in there who sold or traded old baseball cards but most of his stuff was either too old or beat up you couldn't even make out who the player was but still wanted a quarter for it.

The best guy in the whole place was Old Nick who ran a snowcone and popcorn stand by the front entrance. Nick would only charge us kids a dime for a snowcone and everyone else was a quarter.

"Wow! It's good being a kid!"

Getting back to the story – one day Jimmy came running over to our house and told me the news. "That's right, I just heard, The Lone Ranger and Tonto will be in person at Fuzzy's this Saturday afternoon and Joey and me are going!"

Oh My God! In person, in real life, not on TV, not a movie, "Count me in – I'm going too!"

Jimmy told me it costs a whole dollar to see them, so now I have to talk to Mom because Pop is way too cheap to give me a whole dollar! Anyway Saturday comes around, Mom came through like a saint and Jimmy, Joey and me are off to Fuzzy's. Yahoo, Hi-Yo Silver, Buckeroos!

We get there and the parking lot was full, the people were parking all the way over to our street. But with the multitude of human flesh we finaly squeeze our way in to see the Greatest Show on Earth. That's right! The way I thought, it was way better seeing the Lone Ranger and Tonto in person than any old Circus where your constantly stepping in elephant poop.

When we got up to the stage there they were; The Lone Ranger wearing his mask, his famous pair of pearl handled silver six shooters and his white Stetson with his Indian partner, Tonto, wearing his buckskins, his headband and only one gun.

They were smiling and answering some questions from the crowd mostly like other Hollywood stars and what are they like. Then this big man got to the microphone and told everyone if they wanted an autograph on their picture and a memento, the Ranger and Tonto will be at the table by the door and everyone can ask only one question, all for just a $1.00 donation.

Well, we got in line and I'm thinking what's the donation for anyway? Maybe poor Indian Kids? How about doctor bills for the bandits he always shot in the hands to disarm them? I got it, how about, to pay for the cleaners because every show they are both fighting with the bad guys and getting their clothes dirty and afterwards they must change into clean clothes? Hey that's it, that's why they have commercials so they have time to change their clothes after a fight.

Now it's our turn! The big guy tells us all again only one question each. Jimmy is first he asks Tonto, "Which Indian tribe are you from, Apache you know like Geronimo or the Cleveland Indians in the American League?"

Tonto grunts and answers "Comanche." then the big guy takes Jimmy's dollar, gave him a small paper bag and yells next.

Joey's turn, he gets in front of them and starts to give them hand signs, The Ranger looks at Joey signing away looks at Tonto, looks back at Joey, "Whoa! Tonto, you got this one."

Tonto looks at Joey, "Me sorry boy, only know Indian sign language!" then he raises his hand and says, "How!" The crowd laughs and the big guy takes his dollar and gives him his paper bag. Tonto grabs Joey and gives him his dollar back then Joey shakes his hand and everybody claps.

Hmmm. Now if I do some hand signing I won't have to pay either. Na, with my luck I'd get caught and Tonto would probably scalp me. Anyway, The big guy asked me what is your question? The question of all questions that has never been answered correctly since the beginning of time, "What does Kemo-Sabe mean?"

Tonto looked at me right in the eye, smiled and said, "Have to say that, him star, make more money than me – me don't make poo." The crowd laughed, and laughed, and laughed, a couple of men even patted me on the back and the crowd laughed some more like I was a hero or maybe was I a fool. The big guy took my dollar and gave me a bag then yelled next.

So now the three of us are outside sitting on this low wall when Jimmy opens his bag and tells Joey and I to open ours. Holy Cow! I almost forgot about this as I'm tearing the bag open and looking at this 3 by 5 index card with their picture on it and printed on it was, "Best Wishes, The Lone Ranger & Tonto." What? Not even hand signed? Boy oh boy, and I thought my old man was cheap.

Oh now for the memento and the moment of truth, justice and the American way. There it is in the bottom of the bag. I pull it out slowly and I'm almost blinded by the brilliance of the sun coming off this 100% silver bullet made of the shiniest plastic piece of crap I have ever seen in my entire 10 years of living. But here's the most hurtful kick in the butt, it even had MADE IN JAPAN stamped on the bottom.

Evil-Eyed Fleagle

OH Yippie! School days! Here was our routine that we were suppose to follow; First, all of us had to get up at the same time while it was still dark outside, wash up, brush our teeth, use the facilities, just my brother and sister combed their hair – I always had a crew cut or what they call a buzz cut now days. Then get dressed run downstairs grab a bite to eat and off to school. Sounds easy enough, right, think about this we only had one bathroom! My brother was in the 7th grade now so he spent some time in front of the mirror combing his hair to be just right so the girls would hang around him. My sister had long hair that took longer to brush, comb and put ribbons in it while the youngest, you know who, little baby brother in the hallway outside the bathroom door with his eyes and legs crossed was doing the pee-pee dance while knocking on the door!

Now take my brother Hal, he had to leave the house first because he rode the school bus, my sister Oggie and I had to <u>WALK</u> to school which seemed at least 100 miles from our house uphill both ways. Rain, snow, sleet, and probably gloom of night if they could do it to us. That, my friends was our chore for the day.

After you got there you were too tired to think or even open a book let alone learn something. I think for some kids just breathing was hard. I always wanted to sit in the back of the class so I could put my feet up on the empty chair in front of me, except in Mrs. Fleagle's class, we called her Evil Eye Fleagle because of her name was the same as a character in the comic papers and we thought she could see someone doing something even with her back towards us. You could tell she was pissed because she would turn around slowly, look over her coke bottle glasses, snort with steam coming out of her ears and nose just like a bull and walk right to the culprit. Then she motioned for you to stretch out your hand palm down and smack you across your knuckles as hard as that little witch could do with that wooden ruler she always had within reach.

One day Tommy Bigmouth, his real name was Biggans, but we all had nicknames, anyway, Tommy was sitting in the back of the room opposite me along the other side of the room away from the windows. Well, he decided to shoot a spitball at me but missed and of course splattered across a window with a loud thud. Of course everyone roared, Fleagle turned around, told everyone to calm down and walked over to her desk and picked up her ruler. The class was as quiet as a cemetery at midnight on Halloween night. She walked to the middle in the back of the room, looked at the wad on the window dripping down and then looked around the room. Oh man! She doesn't know who did it! Unbelievable! THEN, she walked right over to Tommy, pointed to his hand and WHACK! At that moment Tommy turns red as a beet and yells, "What the hell, you trying to break my damn hand you WICKED EVIL EYED BITCH?" Within a split second she swings a roundhouse with her infamous ruler and breaks it over his head. With steam coming out of her nose like a bull ready to charge, she stomps on the floor and points to Tommy then to the door. We all knew what that meant, it was the signal of all signals – the point that only meant one thing, GO TO THE OFFICE YOUNG MAN!

 Now after she composes herself she goes back to the blackboard and tells the class to lets calm down and get back to what we were doing. At that moment, a small voice from the back of the room over by the window where I was sitting said, "We can all do what we want now evil eye broke her freaking ruler!" She pointed to me with a curled finger and she had the nerve to walk ME right out to the office.

Now, Tommy and I were both in the Office with Fleagle and Mr. Abraham Marksman the Principal of the whole school, and probably the whole world as far as we knew. The Principal was a short, bald, and very stout, I mean, well over 300 pounds who most of the time was looking over his glasses. Meanwhile, after a couple of minutes pacing back and forth while looking out the window he suddenly turned at us shaking his fat head and said, "Well, well, well boys, you two are in a heap of trouble now, Boys." "What to do with you....."

Just then Tommy blurts out, "We didn't do nuttin - it had to be somebody else – Ole Evil Eye Fleagle ain't got no eyes in the back of her freakin head does she?" With that I thought I'll never get out of there alive BUT then the Principal started to smile and had to turn around like he was looking out the window and everyone could see he was laughing even Old Mrs. Feagle.

By then Old Evil Eye stomps her foot on the floor, and screams, "THEY ARE ALL NOTHING BUT BARBARIANS!" Then she storms out of the office, slamming the door behind her. It would have been really cool if the glass in the door shattered just like in the movies but it didn't.

You see, I think there is a moral to this story - the Principal just shook his head while still smiling and told us to sit in the office the rest of the day but he told us we had to write her a note that says we both were sorry and apologize for our actions.

What in the world happened? No telephone calls to our parents, no more broken knuckles, no nothing! We just had to write a stupid dumb letter? Life is GOOD! Oh, By The Way we never did write Old Evil Eye that letter because the following week she left school.

Rumor has it she went total bananas and joined a convent or maybe a traveling circus or something like that. Maybe was put in a mental hospital or was chained up and tortured by hitting her knuckles with a wooden rule and taken some place where nobody could find her – hopefully, like in an old castle dungeon or dried up well!

I also heard from a German kid in one of my classes named Hansel that lived over by Lacey Park who said he heard she bought a ginger bread house that is in the middle of some dark forest and cooks the kids she catches in her old cast iron stove but I really think that, that was a bunch of sauerkraut!

On Today's Lunch Menu, Hoagies!

There was this teacher that I had, Miss Maggie O'Neill, in the 5th grade that everyone liked. She was a young teacher fresh out of college and believed in a reward system and told us about it. She figured if you did well and minded in her class you would be awarded and if you didn't do well or was a problem, no reward for you. She always had a big bowl of fruit on her desk and often used them as rewards if she didn't eat them all herself.

She was only about five foot tall and about the same in width, with long bright red hair, never married and lived with her parents on their big farm on the other side of Ivyland, PA. The only thing that was strange about her was, wait a minute, no, we cannot say strange, how about always hungry, that's better, she loved to eat. It's a good thing her folks had a farm because she could defiantly eat! As a matter of fact, I think that's the only reason why her parents owned a farm.

One day, I think it was in the spring that Miss O'Neill gave us all a permission slip for our parents to sign so the whole class, all 12 of us could go on a field trip for a day to her parent's farm where we can pet the cows, sheep, and goats and see how they raised chickens and ducks. Also she would show us how they planted potatoes, hay and other stuff. We all had to bring a pair of rain boots along with our regular shoes. When I asked about the boots she told me we would probably go in the barn to see the cows getting milked and that their cows are not potty trained if we got her drift. Hmmm, I can see it now, she is going to turn us all into Irish Farmers. Then of course I had to ask, "Ah, Miss O'Neill do we all have to wear bib overalls and a straw hat and chew on a piece of straw?" She only grinned.

The next day everyone turned in our sheets and Miss O'Neill gave only me a sealed envelope to give to my mother and told me to not open it. It was very important! Oh damn! What in God's name did I do now? I know Judy, the girl that used to sit in front of me with the long ponytail that I taped to her chair told on me. Maybe it was Tommy who blamed me when he put some dog poo under Sally's desk. How about me putting the end of Mary's pigtails in the ink well? Or maybe, wait a minute, who cares, why worry!

The Note – That evening when Mom opens it, shakes her head and looks at me. then I start shaking and blurted out, "I didn't do it!"

Mom only said, "How many kids are in your class?"

"Twelve counting me"

"Why would she want 15 of these?"

"Mom what are you talking about?"

"Never mind, I'll call her." Now my mind is wondering, what is that teacher talking about, I didn't do anything 15 times that I can remember and for what matters to every kid in my class? "Mom, what's that all about?"

"It seems your teacher is asking me to make 15 hoagies for your class trip."

"15 hoagies for 12 kids .... wait .... she told us what we were going to do, I guess she must have made her hungry?"

The following week my class went to my teacher's farm and Mom made 10 hoagies cut in half, duh.

When we got there the first stop was in the milking barn where we had to put our boots on and watch where we walked, lesson received – don't worry about stupid cow poop, it's everywhere! Then I asked Miss O'Neill why did we put on our boots and she didn't while we all started to laugh because she was standing in an gigantic cow flop with just her shoes on! "OH, OH! ..."

That was her answer when she slipped and fell on her butt right into another pile of poo.

This was just like an old comedy movie because when she tried to get up she slipped again and again while her dress flew over her head that was now covered completely with the smelly stuff that comes out of a cow's butt. Then slipped head first in the trough full of cow poo. During all this laughing and embarrassment it took two farm hands to get her up. Trust me, after that episode of dung, we all learned 5 things. First - cow poo stinks. Second – it's slippery when its wet. Third – Cows don't care where they do it. Fourth – the moon does come out during the day. Finally the fifth, which is the same as the first and the most important – Cow poop sure does stink!

While our teacher got hosed off, went into the house to wash up and change, the farm hands, Jose and Gus told us all how the milking machines did the milking and that they don't milk them by hand anymore.

Then off to the chicken coop where Miss O'Neill joins us and a couple of girls asked how she was while us guys just snickered. She asked us all not to mention anything about what happened, all the girls just nodded of course and us guys, well, we found out that like I mentioned before that the moon actually does come out during the day. Oh all right, we just smiled.

I only have two comments about farms, chicken coops stink as much if not more than cow barns but the main thing after learning all about chickens is that the eggs come out of the same place as chicken poop! I swear I didn't eat another egg until I joined the Navy when I was 17.

After my stomach was upset at me for bringing it to all these great smells, our teacher tells us that it was lunchtime. Her mother set out a spread for us kids on a couple of picnic tables. On one table she had big bowls of potato salad, macaroni salad, and some other stuff with tiny marshmallows, a bunch of cut up fruit, nuts, and some white creamy stuff all mixed in it and of course that big pile of hoagies cut in half. She also had a tray of hot dogs, a pot of baked beans and pitchers of Kool-Aid, WOW what a feast!

The idea was for everybody to grab a plate and help him or herself. Needless to say everyone knew that Miss O'Neill would be the first to load up her plate and boy I don't really think she would have room for even a pickle. Amazement was not a word but we all just stood there with our mouths open watching her waddle over to the other tables.

Anyway, did you ever notice that if a big person was the only one to sit down on the end of a picnic table bench, does it flip up? You guessed it, when she sat down the bench flipped, the plate of food flew at least 20 feet in the air, our teacher fell on the ground, the food came down all over her, AND when she was getting up her pants ripped right down the seam of her butt! She was crying while running for the house. After that we all ate laughed some more then went home.

That evening my Mom asked me how was the trip to the farm today? I answered her the best I think I could with, "Did you know that only in the farm lands of America that the moon can come out twice and sometimes even more like three times in the daytime?"

Bob Harner

Concrete Impressions
or Maybe Just Tommy's Memorial?

Believe it or not the elementary school I went to back in the 50's is still standing after which I think being built when George Washington was President. Its on Street Road in Warminster, PA and is now some kind of district offices for the school district. When it was a school it held 6 classrooms, one for each grade, a school office and a nurse's room that were all on the main floor with the cafeteria / assembly hall in the basement which had a sign on the doors saying it was also a bomb and fallout shelter.

One day they told us to only use water sparingly in the school because there was something wrong with the well. They brought in these big metal containers into the cafeteria fill of water for us kids. At the same time workmen were outside making forms to pour a concrete slab to hold an enormous water tank which should take a couple of weeks to finish.

In the meantime the teachers drew up a plan for all the kids in the school would put their name and grade on a little card and drop it in a box and afterwards the teachers would pick one name from each of the 6 grades and that winning kid would get to put his or her hand print in the wet concrete just like in Hollywood. After that a teacher would put the student's initials and the date by the imprint.

I think all was going along fine until my class of 5th graders was chosen. Oh Yes, Who's name was pulled? Was it mine? Maybe Johnny's? How about Judy's? It was the one and only, Tommy "Bigmouth" Biggings!

Tommy gets ushered up to the edge of the concrete with a teacher on one side and a construction worker on the other side. They both held him when he stuck his hand on the cement then he got up turned to the crowd and wiped his hands. Then of course, we all clapped and cheered him.

But then when the teachers turned back and looked at the concrete slab with great pride and admiration, one lady teacher gasped with "Oh My God!" Miss O'Neill almost fainted! Mrs. Mayberry the school nurse ran away screaming with most of the girl students and Mr. Howell our only male teacher fell on the ground laughing like hell along with us guys pointing and laughing!

THERE IT WAS, an imprint in all its glory, the Rembrandt of artistry that will live forever in all history, the simple elegance of our own Tommy Bigmouth's bare butt right next to his handprint in the wet concrete! At that time Tommy grabbed a towel, wiped his butt and was pulling his pants up when standing right in front of him was our school principal, old "Mean" Mr. Abraham Marksman!

It took only as fast of a blink of an eye for Old Mean Marksman to grab Tommy by his ear which probably was the only place on him that wasn't covered with cement and as we all wondered why it didn't tear off. Then dragged Tommy around the building and up to his office all the time as Tommy was screaming, "Let go my ear ya fat old bastard!"

In the meantime the concrete workmen told the teachers while trying to hold back from laughing that they would try to fix it but it was a deep imprint and the concrete has set up. To this day, I still think that piece of art should still be there if that concrete pad is there.

Now none of us really know for sure what actually happened but after that incident we didn't see Tommy for about a week in school. As far as I know Tommy never said anything about that whole concrete incident.

In my own truthful opinion – I think that Tommy was only expressing his bottom thoughts about the whole affair!

Camping at the Bass River State Forest

Now here's a story about being invited to go to Bass River State Forest and Lake Absegami that is somewhere in the Pine Barons of New Jersey with my friend, Moe Weinberg, his parents and his, Oh my God, a want-to-be super fashion star, miss princess pain-in-the-butt sister. Moe was my age as we were in the same class in school. His sister Sylvia was about 5 years older than us and was pretty, so she said, but a serious pain. Now I don't really know why but she went to some kind of special school for girls somewhere near Willow Grove where I think they taught her how to be the most irritating and whiny Miss Princess in the world.

Moe's folks had a big Chrysler station wagon from the 1940's with the wooden sides that his father used to wash and wax nearly every weekend. Then he washed Moe's mother's car, a new Cadillac, but he didn't wax it. I think that was an argument with him and her because Moe ended up waxing it but....

Well, he could only do the part he could reach. At that time he was about as tall as me. Now that's another story for another time.

So on this special Friday afternoon after the station wagon was cleaned and polished we loaded as much gear in that wagon as we could and then loaded a small trailer that had the same wood on its sides that made it look like it was part of the car, full of camping gear like tents and stuff so we could leave early the next day.

I had the idea that we were going to build our campsite, log cabin and rough it by chopping down trees and thatching roofs and living Davy Crockett or Daniel Boone style. Well after seeing the tents, the cots, the dining tent, stoves, a shower tent, gas generator, gas cans, four coolers full of Jewish foods like matzo ball soup, gefilte fish, kosher salami and of course a couple loaves of rye bread. Also packed were special maps of New Jersey, the Bass River State Forest and one of the campground we were staying at for the weekend. BUT, the most important thing for just the women, they even had a special tent with just a portable potty in it. After all that I decided definitely to leave my coonskin cap at home.

So after taking two and a half days to pack the ole woody and that trailer we were just about ready to go when Moe's sister asked her father where will she be able to put on her makeup and get ready for a day in the dirty, stinky, wilderness of nowhere? Moe and I looked at each other then looked at his dad when he told her there will be a place for her to do her stuff then turned to us smiled and winked at us. Holy Cow, I think he didn't like her either!

Now it is around 6 A.M. Saturday morning we are all sitting in the woody and starting to pull out of their driveway when – you guessed it. Oh did you ever guess it – it started to rain, I mean downpour, like monsoon time like you see on TV about the jungles of Asia! Now Moe's dad looked at his mom and asked her if she checked the weather report and she said something about that's not her job and if he was so interested in it and bla-bla-bla-bla- she went on like that what seemed forever.

His dad gets out goes back to the house opens the garage door and backs the trailer into the garage then tells Moe and me to - "Well boys wasn't that camping trip fun? Now let's get the trailer unloaded."

Now believe it or not but it took us 2 and a half days to load the station wagon and that trailer but only took about 10 minutes to unload, I guess that was what they call American Ingenuity? Anyway all we did was toss the stuff in the corner of the garage. After that we just stood there in the doorway of the garage watching the pouring rain now with lightning and thunder. Then Moe's father told Moe and I to get in the woody and we drove off to parts unknown, "Happy Trails To You."

Whoa – Hold on, we pulled into the parking lot of my family's restaurant, went in and sat at the counter and Moe's dad said he's buying lunch for us men. Then looks right at me, "What's good on the menu, Bobby?" Well, he didn't need to ask me the second time as I blurted out to my mom, "A cheesesteak with fried onions, pickles and ketchup, french fries and a black and white milkshake!

Moe's dad just smiled and said, "That sounds pretty good, we'll have three of them."

Mom told the cook the order and came back with, "You know my son actually loves the blue plate special, you know a meatloaf platter with mashed potatoes, green beans and a glass of milk," as she winked and was laughing along with Moe's dad and everyone else in the restaurant as she went back in the kitchen.

When she came back out she looked at the three of us and mentioned to Mr. Weinberg that she thought we were all going camping and Moe's dad said only one word, "RAIN" and pointed over his shoulder to the door. Everyone in the whole restaurant looked out the doors and windows and saw not a cloud in the sky, the sun shinning as bright as can be and also a brilliant magnificent bright rainbow.

You know, I think this was the first time that I ever saw a grown man actually cry. After that we all ate our sandwiches and savored our Black and White milkshake with a slice of Mom's homemade lemon meringue pie.

Ice Hockey?

One day in the middle of the coldest week in February about six of us guys decided we were going to play some ice hockey but first we needed equipment. Jimmy, his brother Joey and Moe had their own skates. Timmy had two pairs, the one that he would use had the boot with them and the other that he gave to me to use were the kind you strapped on you shoes like roller skates and with that same key to tighten them. Tommy didn't have any but he said he never knew how to skate anyway so he didn't need them to play the goalie.

All we needed were the hockey sticks now, so off to Fuzzy's Auction House and to see Fuzzy himself. Once there I asked for Fuzzy and here he comes out of a pile of junk all 400 pounds of himself. "What's on your little minds there, kids?"

"You got any hockey sticks?"

"Hmmm ….. Hockey sticks, now where did I put them?" "Oh yeah, over here." he grabs a stick and brushes off the dust, "Here it is, the last one and just for you boys, ten bucks."

Tommy grabs it looks it over real good and, "Yo, it's made out of wood!"

"They are all made of wood, kid."

"I thought it would have been made out of gold with you wanting ten bucks for it."

"Okay, gimme $8 – my final price!"

And then Tommy with his big mouth looks Fuzzy right in the eye and tells him, "For $8 you keep it to hold open the lid in the crate they put you in because they don't make a casket big enough for your fat ass when you croak!" With all of that, we were chased out and told not to come back!

Now there is one point that was made - we still need hockey sticks.

Moe is the second smartest kid around the neighborhood next to me of course, but he still had a good idea. He said find some tree branches in the woods and make them into hockey sticks. Sure and none of us know how to even turn a saw on let alone make a stick.... wait I've got it – my uncle Mike has a little wood shop behind his house! We all agreed and went out into the woods with my brother's genuine Boy Scout hatchet! My brother told me to guard it with my life because if it comes back with a nick in it he would chop my ass off and that would really hurt.

So off to the woods! We all started looking for our own special tree that had a crook or branch coming straight out of the side and just then as being put there by the Hockey Gods of Canada, this was a piece of beauty – better than store bought – yeah I know what you're thinking it's just a stick but I found it and now to chop it down. Now this sapling was about an inch thick, (In arithmetic class at school we called how thick something was it was by its dia…. Oh, what was I thinking, we're in the woods not a classroom!). After a couple whacks even Paul Bunyan up in the north woods could hear that immortal word when we all shouted out, TIMBER!

Now there we were dragging out our trees from the forest and on our way to Uncle Mike's for him to show us how to make our hockey sticks when there is my sister and Mom at our mailbox and with mom shaking her head and hands on her hip says, "What do you have there boys?"

Sticking out our chests like proud peacocks, "We chopped down some wood to make hockey sticks."

"Really, let me see that wood," after looking at our sticks for only a second she told us to put them all over there by the side of the woods then come back here cause she has something for us.

Whoa! We all look at each other, look at our so called wood, look at mom as she's smiling and ran dragging the sticks, throwing the sticks in a pile then running back to mom. She then told us to go in the kitchen. Mom told all six of us to wash our hands real good and she even washed Hal's genuine Boy Scout hatchet. After our wash down she looked at our arms and told us we were having some ice cream while she makes a phone call.

Now I'm a little confused, get rid of our sticks, the wash down, ice cream for all, now she has to make a call? I get it! OH NO! We cut down some special trees that the forest rangers or Arbor

Day people planted because those plants were on the endangered list. My mom is turning us in to the tree cops – my whole life ruined just because we wanted to play hockey.

After our ice cream, Mom looks at our arms again. She said everyone was clear but it can happen because …. then I blurted out special endangered trees right? Mom looked at me and shook her head, "No, those so-called trees were Poison Sumac." "Now, I called all your moms and you all go home a get a bath so you don't get any rashes. And you young man, upstairs and in the tub, then clean clothes."

Later on while at dinner, "Boy, I'm glad I won't be going to jail."

Then my sister, "Mom, what in the world is my stupid little brother talking about now, everyone knows you don't go to jail for getting poison sumac."

"Eat your dinner, Oggie."

WOW!

A Brand New, Second Handed TV!

There were so many times my father proved his holy cheapness, like in 1956 the old man went to a place called Fuzzy's Auction House and Emporium in Warminster on Old York Road where they sell and auction off used junk, oops, I mean previously used reconditioned junk. When he got home his chest was sticking out like a proud peacock proclaiming that we were the first in the neighborhood to get a brand new, second handed and slightly used 1931 Western Television set that was made by the Echophone Co, twenty some years earlier. This 5 ton set actually had a screen that was about 6 or 8 inches with a diagonal 18 inch by 4 inch thick magnifying glass hung in front of it that took pop a couple of hours to figure out how to put it on. This is when everyone else in the world were talking about their new Admiral's, Crosby's, RCA's or Philco's with their 24 inch screens. Now, do not think for one moment that we were not ungrateful but to see a clear picture you had to sit directly in front and get your sister to almost stand on her head while holding the rabbit ear antenna.

That was only one of many reasons we called the old man his holy cheapness as he was a deacon in our Reformed Baptist

Church where all of us had to go every Sunday from 9 in the morning to probably only The Grim Reaper himself knew when. At the end of the main service the old man and another Deacon would go up the two aisles and pass the collection basket back and forth to each other and if my old man heard change hit the bottom of the basket he'd give that stern look over his glasses. No sound in the basket meant someone put the stuff what he called cotton money cause paper doesn't make a sound when you drop it in and would yell, "Thank You Jesus, Thank You Lord!"

It's funny though, every Sunday after the service the Pastor would always take the old man to the side and wiggle his finger in his face. I really never knew if he was getting yelled at or thanked but I do know that his cheapness would drop some loose change, mainly pennies in an envelope and put that in the basket. Now don't get me wrong, sometimes the sun did shine on us because sometimes after the main services we could go home with mom supposedly to help her make dinner. When he asked her if we were really going to help her, she would just smile.

Getting back to his holy cheapness – on this one particular Wednesday evening some of the neighborhood kids which weren't many, came over, believe it or not, to watch our antique TV because Disney was on and there was a serial on that show of the Greatest Show Ever!

The One – The Only – Davy Crockett! There we were huddled around the infamous magnifying glass with our coonskin caps on and singing all the words to "the Ballad of Davy Crockett." Actually I think the main reason the kids came to watch the show at our house is not our famous TV but because mom always had snacks for all of us like popcorn, chips, pretzels and of course ice cold cherry Kool Aid.

Now, his holy cheapness had this brain fart that he could hold a mini bible class for us kids during the commercials wasn't bad enough and what the hell did he actually think that a bunch of kids would want to go to bible school on a Wednesday night instead of watching DAVY CROCKETT! It wasn't all that bad really for we talked over him except for Moe and Donald who went in the other room because Moe was a Jew and Donald was a Jehovah's Witness. The worst part of the whole evening happened during the final TV commercial - His Holy Cheapness passed around a collection plate to be donated to the orphan kids over at Christ Home. I often wondered to this day after that night about the true meaning why the neighborhood kids didn't come back.

Also in the early 50's there was a new show on TV called, "The Adventures of Superman", starring George Reeves who I thought would have bulging muscles like in the comic books but then what do I know, I was a gullible kid. He had super powers so he didn't need big muscles. Remember at the beginning of each show, "Faster then a speeding bullet, stronger than a locomotive and able to leap tall buildings with a single bound, and on and on." He always saved Lois Lane and Jimmy in the nick of time from the bad guys and never even flinched when they shot their guns at him but he ducked if they threw their guns at him.

Most of us kids would tie something around our necks that we could use as a cape and run around pretending to be a super hero. This was fun and one time I decided to tie an old blanket around my neck and jump out of my bedroom window on the second floor into a pile of sand but Mom stopped all the fun and that idea after she found out. My next one was with a pillowcase as a cape jumping from the top of a big stuffed chair that was in the living room. Let me tell you that didn't work out too good either. A cracked arm bone later hurt like hell but I got a cast on my arm and didn't have to go to Sunday school for four weeks because I couldn't put my suit coat on over the cast. Here's the worse part of it all, I did have to go to school even with the cast on.

At school I was now the hero of the class because every kid wanted to sign their name or some saying on my cast. The main thing was since all we had were pencils an not pens after about two weeks the lead from the pencils became smudged and unreadable so I decided to wash off that dirty mess. By the way, let me tell everyone that water and a Plaster of Paris cast is not meant to be used in the same sentence, which actually means I had to go back to Dr. Camel's for another cast. He was no fun at all because he put a new kind of a removable plastic one on my arm. Kinda takes all the fun out of it, but at least I still didn't have to go to Sunday school for two more weeks.

With that in mind His Holy Cheapness, my Pop said he should take it upon himself to instruct me about the stories in the Bible and of the works of the Lord at home since I can't make it to Sunday School. He used to mumble something else about he should write a letter to the TV station about putting that trash on TV and telling children to believe in super powers and things that aren't real in life. Sometimes he has said that he should have never bought that TV because of the way it influences the minds of the young.

Mom told him to leave me alone because every show on TV is supposed to be entertainment, make believe, and fun except for the news because she thinks that's just all made-up hype. (All right, Mom!)

In my own opinion after all of that stuff about Superman's super-powers and saving the same dumb people every week most of us kids started to wear our coon skinned caps again while watching TV and singing the song about Davy Crockett, "King of the Wild Frontier."

The Birds and the Bees!

As I mentioned before the school I went to only had six classrooms with each grade from one through six having their own classroom. So beginning in first grade and continuing for the next five years every class we were in the teachers always assigned us kids to sit in their classes alphabetically and sitting either next to me, behind me or in front of me was Judith Hallowitz who everyone called Judy.

Judy was either the smartest kid in the class always getting A's and always doing her homework. Maybe she was the daughter of the principal or a teacher or maybe Einstein himself. She had very long hair like down to the middle of her back and one Monday she came in with her hair cut real short.

A lot of the kids made fun of her haircut and of course I felt sorry for her, told her it looked good and you guessed it – SHE KISSED ME ON THE CHEEK! Whoa, we were in the third grade then and after that all the kids were teasing me about her and she even tried to hang around with me the rest of that year.

In fourth grade we both had our desks next to each other again. Now our fourth grade teacher came up with the idea to put on a play or something like that and of course you know that Judy had the lead role. She also asked the teacher to get me to play her husband if it was going to be a play! At that time I'm about 9 or 10 years old and didn't want NO part of any type of play or even her at all. The teacher in turn got Moe Weinberg to play that part and YES I was off the hook. Moe and Judy became friends easily because as we found out they were both Jewish which didn't mean anything to me but I really can't think of any other reason. Then all the teachers decided that us kids would recite nursery rhymes instead of that play, that's right, the whole fourth grade would get up on stage and say one rhyme apiece. Instead of a piece from some Shakespeare play. The teachers thought that it would be too difficult for fourth graders. I think it wouldn't have been too hard but who the hell talks like Shakespeare anyway?

At the show Grasso was first to go on and Moe was the emcee. Grasso stood about 4 foot nothing but came in on the scale at least 300 pounds. Being Italian decent his real name was Antonio but his older brother nicknamed him Grasso which I was told means, "Fatty" in Italian. His rhyme was "Jack and Jill" and it went something like this, " Jack and his-a girlfriend day go up dis-a hill you know and they gets some-a-thing in a bucket. Now she done comma down a-crying causes-a dare was-a hole in da bucket. He bowed and started to sing ,"OOH my bucket gotta hole in it – my bucket.... Now that student body along with the teachers and visitors were laughing, praising us and hollering, "Bravo!" Whatever that meant.

Next up was, "Squirt," that was me. First of all I was shortest in the 4th grade but NOOOO! My brother Hal gave it to me from when we were in the caverns at the south end of the skyline drive. Anyway my rhyme was "Ole Mother Hubbard". "Ole mother Hubbard went to the cupboard to get her poor dog a bone, when she got there the cupboard was bare so the dog ate HER." "Her dog was actually a lion because she was nearsighted."

Now a couple of teachers were saying they didn't have anything to do with that and walked out. The principal got up and commended us for thinking up something so humorous while looking at his pocket watch. I'm sorry we cannot continue our program because it is getting late and call it a day.

On another day in about late October our school handed out little containers that looked like little milk cartons but they were sealed shut with a slot on the top so you could use them as banks. How clever only trouble I didn't have anything left to put in it after getting my quarter once a week from picking up the trash at the restaurant. Ooops! I didn't tell you that those milk cartons had "Please Give To UNICEF" in big letters all over them. We were all told that when we went out on Halloween night while trick or treating we were supposed to ask everyone to donate their loose change to this worthy cause. Now Judy told me if I opened the carton I would go to HELL! Of all people to tell me that when her folks won't let her go out on Halloween. Anyway that was something to think about. Hmmm, maybe Jewish people have a different Hell than where my old man says I'm going?

On Halloween the only trouble was that some people when shown the milk carton and we were told, "Hey kid you want some pennies or the candy?"

What an easy question. I put the milk carton in my bag grinned then held out the bag and answered with "Trick or Treat!"

Well, I did my duty and the day after turned the milk carton in to my teacher and she put our names on them. A couple days later after that she told the class who collected the most money and he or she got a gold star. Whoopie doo! That was Timmy, but he lived in Ivyland where all the gazillions of houses were close together.

A couple of kids didn't turn in anything and Miss Smarty Pants Judy was one of them – After a few weeks passed her family moved out of town because we were told her father was in the Military and got stationed someplace else. Or, maybe they just took the money and moved to Hawaii or Australia or some other far place where nobody knew them? You figure it out – I think I know, who is going to Hell now?

As I grow older I do realize that the large majority of boys at 9 or 10 years old are hardly into girls that much. So how come in about 3 or 4 years later for that matter how old we get, we can't stop thinking of them?

Thanksgiving with my Family
or just plain... "LOOK OUT!" HERE THEY COME!

As far as I can remember our extended family on my mother's side came over for Thanksgiving. Our German Uncle Gus and Aunt Olga who my sister was named after lived in Fishtown that is part of Philadelphia but I didn't really think it was named from the smell of fish. Uncle Johnny and his brood of 2 kids lived in South Philly. His wife, Marion was Italian and made the best spaghetti known to all. Also was my Uncle Nicky with Aunt Dotsy and their kids Little Nicky, Patsy and Davy. They also lived somewhere in Philly. To this day I have no idea why all Uncle Nicky's tribe names ended in Y? Now every Thanksgiving they all showed up for dinner or just wanted to get out of the city but they were family, I think.

The normal ritual for dinner is kids in the kitchen at the kid's table and the adults in the dinning room. My brother was the oldest kid so he was suppose to do like Uncle Gus said "Ya, you be keeper of an orderly ship, ya?" Most of us actually never understood him.

Mostly every man ate and ate until they undid their belts sat back in their chairs and belched. Of course all the aunts grunted with "MEN!"

All the women started clearing the table off and trying to decide if to have dessert now or wait awhile. Us kids went in the living room and the men folks gather around the part of the table that was cleared. And then IT HAPPENED! Old cheap master of the feast made the announcement he made every year while going over to the china cabinet unlocking the door that hasn't been opened since last year, then getting the old famous bottle of Napoleon Brandy that was as dusty and smelled like the cat's box. They all smiled, nodded their heads and sat there in awe as the old man pour a shot for each of them. This ritual of the shot was going on every year for as long as I can remember.

Uncle Nicky was the first with his shot downing it in one gulp then yelling, "DAM THAT SHIT WENT BAD!" while running out to his car and back in with his own half gallon bottle of 'Ole Crow Whiskey' while the rest of them just stood there with their mouths wide open.

Now they are all sniffing the brandy and shaking their heads while Nicky is pouring out the Whiskey in water glasses and passing them around while uttering "Lets have a man's drink for the holiday instead of that rat's piss!"

You have to remember my old man a Deacon of the Church never lets alcohol touch his lips except for communion wine and Thanksgiving and now instead of a shot, a whole big freaking water glass full and them making him drink it all. Whoa, I never saw anyone get plastered that fast as my old man and it took two guys to drag his drunken ass up to bed with mom bringing a bucket up right behind them while mumbling, "I'm not going to clean up that!"

After all that commotion we had cherry pie, apple pie, pumpkin pie and even minced meat pie, whatever that is, sat around the living room laughing, talking and of course the men drinking Uncle Nicky's whiskey. Uncle Gus then pointing upstairs and hearing the old man moaning told all us kids, "Oh mein Gott, Gott getting even mit him fer trying to drink das in eins gulp!"

Aunt Olga – "You can always tell when Gus had a few, he starts talking half in German and the rest in something nobody can understand."

"Hmm, that's an idea, I don't speak German so maybe I don't have to listen."

"Want another *Krombacher, Uncle Gus?"
(*One of the top German beers.)

December means
THE CHRISTMAS SCHOOL
BREAK!

To those who don't remember these things that happened to most kids in December, its when Mom took Hal, Oggie and me on the train early one day to Philadelphia where all those big department stores are like Gimbles, Lit Brothers, Strawbridges who by-the-way don't sell strawberries, and of course Wanamakers that I was told was the oldest and biggest department store in the world. Really, it's big but the world is bigger than my brain could imagine that anything is bigger.

I think the real reason for this trip is that we get a cool train ride all the way to downtown big ass city so Mom can buy us some clothes for Christmas and we can see all the places that are decked out for the holiday. Hal says bull...t its so Mom has someone to carry her bags of stuff she bought around all day.

Now on just about every corner of the sidewalks outside there is a man in a Santa Claus suit ringing a bell with a black pot

85

hanging from what I think may be a camera's stand hollering Merry Christmas, Merry Christmas. I asked Mom "What the .." she cut me off and said, "They are Santa's helpers."

I said "If they are helpers why aren't they elves instead of dirty old men that smell like wine and cigars?"

Most of the time my sister wanted to just look at the fancy girl clothes in the store windows. Hal and I liked the sporting goods department but to tell the truth I liked the toy stuff. You know that Wanamakers had a whole floor with just toys in it. Boy it would take me like forever to see all that stuff but Mom said "Come on kids its almost lunch time, we can look at the toys later."

Well that's a word that has no meaning, you know LATER!

For lunch we went to this big place called Horn and Hardluck or something like that they had all these little doors on the walls with sandwiches to pieces of pies and cakes and a cafeteria style line like in school where you could get anything that you wanted like when my brother pointed and said, "Look squirt they have your favorite a Blue Plate Special!"

Mom smiled and told him not to pick on me. Anyway I got a Cheeseburger and fries with a black and white shake but didn't have any room left for that big piece of lemon meringue pie.

While we were eating about 8 people dressed in some old fashion clothes with the men wearing those tall hats started to sing Christmas Carole's right at our table. They even sang "Rudolph the Red Nosed Reindeer" to us kids and to my full stomach's surprise we were handed a candy cane and told

Merry Christmas. Then everyone in the place clapped. To this day I don't know if they clapped because we got candy canes or because they quit singing and walked away. My opinion was probably of them going away because they sounded more like a couple of tomcats fighting to me.

After all that it was back to shopping, looking at windows dressed up for the season. Then to Gimbels last because it was next to the train station. Now my legs were tired of walking and my arms were ready to fall off from toting two bags that I think had 100-pound cannon balls in them. Worst of all it's starting to snow and we had a half of block to go which seemed like a mile up hill. I now had enough shopping for my entire life!

Our train ride home was uneventful because the windows kept fogging up but there was an old lady sitting across from us asking about our day shopping that my brother and myself felt like stuffing a scarf in her mouth – she talked all the way from the city to the Willow Grove station where she finally got off. You know it wasn't just my brother and I who thought she was a pain but when she got off everyone clapped.

Its still December and now its our Old Man's time to torment us.

The three of us guys, (The Old Man, Brother Hal and myself), are going to what the old man says is the Great White North to cut down two Christmas trees just like our forefathers did, one for the restaurant the other for home.

Two days prior our Old Man spent time sharpening a special hand saw that he says cuts live trees the best and wet stones an axe while my brother honed his genuine famous chromed Boy

Scout hatchet. Me, I spent all my time searching for my trusty, rusty Swiss Army penknife with 14 different tools in it including a fork and spoon that my uncle Gus gave me. Duh, It was in my fishing tackle box with some worms that were hard and mummified from sitting in that box for 6 or so months.

Don't laugh because you may never know what a smart kid can do with his old, trusty, rusty Swiss Army penknife with 14 different tools in it including a fork and spoon that my uncle Gus gave me, besides getting Lock-Jaw, whatever that is?

Okay back to this story – the three of us were up way before the sun even thought of rising and on the road in the old Ford. We must have been driving a long time because I took a little nap and when I woke up we were in a town called Bethlehem.

"Holy Cow! How did we get here?"

"What are you yelling about, Squirt?"

"Look at the road side its just 10 miles to Bethlehem – That's God's country!!"

Pop looked in his mirror shook his head motioned, "Ahh, we turn here and a mile up this lane is the tree farm."

I'm totally bonkers now so I just sit back, and there it was an enormous pine tree forest for miles probably all the way to the Alaska. We turned onto a dirt road by the billboard sign that read, "Santa's Tree Farm – Best Trees this Side of the North Pole – You or I will cut them – One Dollar a Foot."

Boy, now I see why we went half way around the world for a tree – only a buck a foot! El Cheapo struck again.

When we pulled up to the barn this man's name should be Paul Bunyan by the size of him. "Yup, Lookin fer a tree are ya?"

"Oh how about one 6 footer and another about 5 foot"

"You be cutting or me?"

"Oh we are." Then the old man opens the trunk and LO and Behold, laying on an old dirty blanket, my trusty, rusty, old Swiss Army penknife with 14 different tools in it including a fork and spoon that my uncle Gus gave me. No Special saw for live trees and genuine famous chrome plated Boy Scout hatchet and no axe. The old man looked at Hal, Hal looked at me then we and even Paul Bunyan looked at my Swiss Army Knife.

"Damn there feller I done figger you's be here till after Christmas tryin to cut down two trees with dat darn thing." We all looked at my Swiss Army and then Hal, Me and the tree man laughed except our cheap Old Man, he showed a tear.

"I'll tell ya what I'll give ya a 6 and a 5 footer fer just 10 bucks cause it be Chistmas time but if I cut them I gots to charge ya 2 bucks exter fer each one." "Dat will be `$14 bucks total." Then with a big grin showing about two teeth in his whole mouth, "Ya know a beaver could knock down 2 trees fer nuttin before you even get the bark off of one with that thing but come to think about dat is I be fresh out of beavers!"

With that he slapped his leg, laughed, spit out some tobacco juice and said, "Damn dat's a good one, I should write it down."

After hearing all that, pop shook his head picked out the trees while the tree guy took his chain saw over to them and in less than a minute had them cut and put on the top of the Old Ford.

Now the next thing that happened while Hal and I an had to turn around so that pop didn't see us laughing when our old man went to pay him he ask him if he had any rope and he told him $3.00 more for 20 feet and a $3.00 tip if he wanted him to tie them down. Pop gave him just the money for the rope and we tied them.

When we were done the tree guy told pop, "Nice doing business with you'll, Merry Christmas To Ya!"

Now here we are on our way home and going down this narrow farm road was a farm tractor pulling a tremendous load of hay doing about 10 miles an hour, pop beeps the horn once, waits then beeps again looks for when the road is straight and puts the peddle to the metal on the old Ford zips around the hay wagon and then 'IT' happened, the worst thing since the Zeppelin Hindenburg Disaster, "Oh the Humanity!"

The rope holding the trees broke, the trees fell on the road and the farm tractor ran right over both of them. The Old man slams on the breaks the framer slams on the tractor breaks, the hay, that's right the hay flies over the tractor an buries the old Ford.

After we dig out from under the hay the farmer looks at pop shaking his head. The Old man yells at the farmer, "Look what you caused with your stupid hay wagon and my Christmas trees ruined!"

"How about my hay who's going to put my hay back on the wagon?

After yelling back and forth another disaster, all of a sudden the

farmer punched pop right in the nose just while a policeman walked up from around the hay pile.

"Now what's going on here?"

Our old man while holding his nose pointing at the farmer, "He caused all this, ran over my kids Christmas trees, buried us with hay and punched me in the nose!"

"And your story, Zeke?" Oh No, the farmer and the cop know each other – Pop's a deadman.

"Well Officer Tom, its like this, this here speed demon with kids in the car, mind you, come flying around me while I was taking it easy form my hay field going to my cow pasture right here." "He then whipped in front of me with these trees on top of his car that he said were tied down, Let me tell you a blind one armed monkey could tie those trees down better than that. Then when they fell off right in front of me, it happened so fast I couldn't help but run over those damn trees when he slammed on his breaks. I then slammed on mine and my hay broke lose."

"And His Nose?"

"Well now you know Officer Tom, I'm a church going Christian and don't go with a lot of yelling and cussing especially with kids around and by God I had to shut him up."

"Ok here's how we are going to do this, first, you two shake hands, second, you and you two kids push this hay off the street; third, Zeke, I'll take you back to your place get your Son Clem to help you to get the hay on your wagon."

"Now wait a minute, Tom…"

"There isn't any wait a minute, here's the fourth option." "I arrest both of you and charge each with Disorderly Conduct, and Disturbing the Peace which will be a Hundred Dollar fine each!" "Well?"

"But that damn farmer punched me in the nose," "That's Assault and Battery!"

"Okay then men, I'll charge Zeke with Assault and Battery and to be fair I'll charge you, Mr. Harner for Wreckless Driving with minors in the car, which both will be another hundred dollar fine each."

They looked at one another and both shook hands!

After all that it was an uneventful ride home except for we still didn't have any Christmas trees and he was quiet and just rubbing his nose. But when we did get home mom asked him, "Well look at the three of you, where's the trees and what's all the hay all over you and your face?"

Pop looked at her right in the eye and answered quickly with, "We forgot the saw and axe then had to look for someone to help us to cut them and we tripped and fell in the hay barn while looking for the someone that worked at the tree farm."

"You know I think this was one of the worse days I ever had."

Hal and I agreed we would never tell the real story but there are two things to get off my chest.

One, is that in the Ten Commandments someplace isn't there a Commandment, 'Thou Shall not Lie'. "At least I'm safe there, I think! I'm not going to Hell for a lie that big!"

"Two, moving the hay off the road I think I lost my old trusty, rusty Swiss Army penknife with 14 different tools in it including a fork and spoon that my uncle Gus gave me."

"Therefore, no worries like what I've been told about getting either lock-jaw, unlock-jaw, tetanus or maybe some kind of jungle fever?"

"Thanks!"
"There's a whole lot more coming soon!"

Bob Harner

www.ingramcontent.com/pod-product-compliance
Lightning Source LLC
Chambersburg PA
CBHW060953040426
42445CB00011B/1133